Taking Visual Impairment to School

by Rita Whitman Steingold

D0521672

Taking Visual Impairment to School
© 2004 JayJo Books
Edited by Karen Schader

Published by
JayJo Books
A Brand of The Guidance Group
Publishing Special Books for Special Kids®

JayJo Books is a publisher of books to help teachers, parents, and children cope with chronic illnesses, special needs, and health education in classroom, family, and social settings.

Library of Congress Control Number: 2004102588
ISBN 10: 1-891383-27-2
ISBN 13: 978-1-891383-27-4
First Edition
Seventeenth book in our *Special Kids in School*® series

For all information, including
Premium and Special Sales, contact:
JayJo Books
The Guidance Group
www.guidance-group.com

The opinions in this book are solely those of the author. Medical care is highly individualized and should never be altered without professional medical consultation.

Dedication

To my students who have inspired me to have vision far beyond sight
To the memory of my parents who instilled within me the need
to care about all living things, especially children

A special thank you to

Karen Schader, my editor

Maria Schauer
Teacher of the Visually Impaired
Certified Orientation and Mobility Specialist
Private consultant in SE Phoenix, Arizona

Iris Torres, Coordinator
Vision Technology Center
NYC Department of Education

Dr. Laurence Gardner, Director
Educational Vision Services
NYC Department of Education

My husband, children, and grandchildren, for all their help and support

Note from the Author
I am a retired New York City and State licensed and certified teacher of the visually impaired. For twenty-five years, I taught at the Queens Center for Multiple Handicapped Children in Little Neck, NY. Today, I am a writer and presenter of classroom workshops in elementary schools: "Introduction to Braille—How the Blind Learn to Read and Write." The workshops not only educate but they are fun for children of all ages!

You may contact me at RWS3460@aol.com.

—Rita Whitman Steingold

Hi, my name is Lisa. I live with my mom, my dad, and my sister Maggie in a brick house with three steps in front. In our garden, there are a lot of flowers that smell really pretty and birds that sing all day long. I love to smell the flowers and hear the birds, but I can't see them because I am blind.

Blindness is a kind of visual impairment, which means a person's eyes just don't work right. I was born blind. Some children are born with sight and become blind because of an accident or sickness.

That doesn't happen too often!

You may know some kids who wear eyeglasses to help them see the chalkboard or read. Some kids, like my friend Pete, have what is called "low vision." They need more than just eyeglasses to help them see. Pete has to sit at the front of the class to see the board. He needs books with large print and magnifying lenses to help him read.

Visual impairment means a lot of different things!

When I was a very little girl, a teacher came to our house to help me learn to use my other senses—hearing, smell, taste, and especially touch. She told my parents and me that I had ten little "eyes" at the end of my fingers and that I would learn all about the world with them. She was right!

Mom and Dad tell me I can learn to do almost anything children with sight do. I even learned to roller-skate down the driveway. When I feel and hear the rough sidewalk under my skates, I know I'm at the end of our driveway and I turn around.

Guess what other "sense" I use a lot? My common sense!

At first, I didn't like to go to school, because I was the only kid in my class who was blind. All the other children were beginning to read, and I wanted to read too. Then Ms. Winkler, a teacher of the visually impaired, started to work with me every day. She told me all about Braille and how it was like a secret code!

Many years ago, Louis Braille, who was blinded as a young boy, figured out a different way to write the alphabet so people could read even if they could not see. He used a thin metal point to push out six tiny dots on paper, close together so that he could feel them with his fingertips. For each letter of the alphabet, the six dots are in different positions.

Here is what my name looks like in Braille. The first dot changes *l* into *L*.

I use a Braillewriter to do my schoolwork. It's a machine that has a special keyboard to print out Braille dots. There's a program that makes my computer "talk," so I can use it to write or work on the Internet. I can even learn to play a musical instrument and read notes in Musical Braille.

Ms. Winkler helps Mr. Brady, my classroom teacher, plan lessons for me and the other kids who are visually impaired. He gives Ms. Winkler the stories, pictures, and maps for our lessons. Then she prints them out in Braille for me and makes them darker or bigger for the kids who have low vision.

I have to practice over and over again to read Braille quickly.

When I first started school, I needed a teacher's aide to be my sighted guide. She would help me find the bathroom, the lunchroom, and the gym. Now, I can go all by myself, because I remember where all the rooms are…it's like I have a "visual map" in my head.

Have you ever seen a person who is blind walking with a white cane? Mr. Ruderman, an orientation and mobility specialist, gave me one. He teaches me how use it in school and around the neighborhood. When I'm walking, I move my cane from side to side…that's called "sweeping." If I hit something, like a trash can, I know to walk around it.

When I'm much older, I want to get a guide dog to help me get around. I'd really like to have a dog!

Every morning, I get washed and dressed by myself. I remember where my mom puts my clothes in the closet and the drawers. Mom types Braille labels for each hanger to let me know the color of my pants, dress, blouse, or sweater. She does the same for my shoes in the bottom of my closet, and for my underwear and socks in my drawers.

I'm even faster at getting dressed than Maggie is…and she's older!

In the bathroom, everything stays in the same place, so I can find my toothbrush, toothpaste, and cup. I don't even need a mirror to comb my hair. Just by feeling my hair, I know if it's smooth the way I like it.

At breakfast, Mom tells me, "The toast's on the right and the jelly's on the left, and your glass of milk is above the plate." Maggie likes to use the numbers on the face of a clock instead. She says, "The toast's at three o'clock, jelly's at nine o'clock, and milk is at noon."

Eating is easy, as long as I'm told what's on the plate and where it is.

My best friends are Julie and Kate. Sometimes we go bowling or play in the house. We also like to watch TV or go to the movies. Of course, I don't see the pictures the way they do, but I have a very good imagination. I see the pictures in my head, just like I do when my dad reads a story to me at bedtime.

Julie and Kate help me when I need it. On the playground at school, Julie says, "Lisa, the swing on your right is empty. You can go on it now." Once we went on a trip to the zoo. Kate told me the colors of the animals, how tall they were, and if they were furry or not.

I even had a ride on a camel. That was scary…and fun!

In the summertime, I go to a camp for kids who are visually impaired. Swimming in the pool is the most fun. Here's how I know I am getting near the end of the pool—I count the strokes! We play baseball too. You might think it's hard for me to play baseball, but guess what...

We use a baseball that beeps, so I can tell where it is by the sound!

On school days, I take my backpack and my white cane and head out the door to get on the school bus with all the other kids. I learn my lessons, have fun with my friends, and do my homework after school. Sometimes, I even go to the school library and check out Braille books by myself—I love to read books!

When I'm all grown up, I'm going to be a teacher, or a lawyer, or a writer, but I have plenty of time to decide. For now, I'm going to play with my friends. See ya!

LET'S TAKE THE KIDS' QUIZ!

1. **What senses does Lisa uses?**
Without the sense of sight, Lisa uses her senses of touch, hearing, smell, and taste to learn about the world. She also uses her common sense!

2. **How does Lisa know she is at the end of the driveway when she is roller-skating?**

Lisa feels and hears the rough sidewalk under her skates. Then she knows it's time to turn around.

3. **What is Braille?**
Braille is a system that people who are blind can use to read and write. It was invented by a man named Louis Braille, who was blind. He pushed out six tiny dots in different positions for each letter, close together so that people could feel them with their fingertips.

4. **What is a Braillewriter?**
A Braillewriter is a machine that has a special keyboard to print out Braille dots.

5. **How does Lisa find her way around school?**
At first, she had a teacher's aide to help her. Once she learned her way, she just remembered, as if she had a visual map in her head.

6. What is "sweeping"?
People who are blind move, or "sweep," their canes from side to side to check for objects in their path.

7. How does Lisa know the color of her clothing?
Lisa's mom types Braille labels and puts them on each item of clothing.

8. At breakfast, if Maggie told Lisa, "Your toast is at three o'clock," what would Lisa do?
She would reach for her toast on the right side of her plate.

9. How can kids who are blind play baseball?
Kids who are blind use a baseball that beeps, so they can tell where it is.

10. What does Lisa want to do when she grows up?
Lisa may decide to be a teacher, a lawyer, or a writer.

TEN TIPS FOR TEACHERS

✓ 1. BE PREPARED.
If this is the first time you have a student who is visually impaired in your class, you may feel concerned. Before the child arrives, read school records and talk with parents, previous classroom teachers, the teacher of the visually impaired (TVI), and other support personnel.

✓ 2. BE PATIENT AND TALK NATURALLY.
It takes time to get to know a new student and for the child to become acquainted with you. Do not hesitate to use words such as "see" and "look" when speaking to a student who is visually impaired. And don't be surprised if, at the end of the school day, the child says, "See you tomorrow" and waves goodbye!

✓ 3. INTRODUCE THE NEW STUDENT.
As with any new child in the classroom, the student who is visually impaired should meet classmates and staff in a pleasant and friendly manner. Encourage other students to say their names, and avoid any "guess who this is" games.

✓ 4. PLAN FOR SPECIAL SUPPLIES AND EQUIPMENT.

A student who is visually impaired may need special supplies or equipment: bookstands, felt tip pens, Braille books, a Braillewriter, computer, tape recorder, etc. If a student needs large print or Braille books, the TVI will order them. Orders are placed in advance of the school year, so the supplies and equipment will be available when the student enters your classroom.

✓ 5. MAKE SURE THE STUDENT HAS A TOUR OF THE SCHOOL.
If the school building is new to the student, it is important to take a "tour" and locate the bathroom, lunchroom, main office, auditorium, gym, etc. The TVI or the orientation and mobility specialist is responsible for teaching the student how to avoid obstacles in the halls, use staircases, and get to and from the classroom independently.

✔ 6. EXPECT THE STUDENT TO FOLLOW RULES.

Just like a child who is sighted, a student who is visually impaired is a member of the school community and should be expected to follow building regulations. In the classroom, as well, the child should learn the teacher's rules and be treated like any other student.

✔ 7. ARRANGE FOR APPROPRIATE SEATING AND STORAGE.

A student with low vision may need assistive devices, such as a magnifier, high intensity lamp, reading stand, and a seat close to the board. A child who is blind needs to have easy access to adaptive aids—Braillewriter, computer, tape recorder, etc. Since some of these items may take extra space, additional storage, such as an extra desk or shelf, may be needed.

✔ 8. BE AWARE OF SAFETY IN THE CLASSROOM.

The student who is visually impaired should be encouraged to explore the classroom, learning where to hang clothes and find books and materials. To avoid accidents, leave doors and closets either fully opened or closed. Also, if changes are made in the position of furniture, such as cabinets, tables, or chairs, the child should be told and shown the new placement. In advance of any emergency, discuss contingency plans for such situations.

✔ 9. MODIFY INSTRUCTIONAL MATERIALS, AS NEEDED.

The TVI will assist you in modifying instructional materials to meet the student's visual needs. In consultation with the TVI, you may wish to use your creative talents to make modifications as well.

✔ 10. TAKE A TEAM APPROACH.

Encourage the parents and caregivers of a student who is visually impaired to become involved in the child's school activities. When adults work as a team, the student has the best opportunity to reach academic and social goals in school and to succeed in life.

ADDITIONAL RESOURCES

American Foundation for the Blind
11 Penn Plaza, Suite 300
New York, NY 10001
212-502-7661
212-502-7662 TTY
800-232-5463
www.afb.org

The American Printing House for the Blind
1839 Frankfort Avenue
P.O. Box 6085
Louisville, Kentucky 40206-0085
800-223-1839
www.aph.org

Association for Education and Rehabilitation of the Blind and Visually Impaired
1703 N. Beauregard Street, Suite 440
Alexandria, VA 22311
877-492-2708
www.aerbvi.org

Helen Keller National Center for Deaf-Blind Youths and Adults
141 Middle Neck Road
Sands Point, NY 11050
516- 944-8900, Ext. 326 (voice/TTY)
www.hknc.org

Lighthouse International
111 East 59th Street
New York, NY 10022-1202
212-821-9200
212-821-9713 TTY
800-829-0500
www.lighthouse.org

National Library Service for the Blind and Physically Handicapped (NLS)
Library of Congress
101 Independence Ave, SE
Washington, DC 20540
800-424-8567
www.loc.gov/nls

To order additional copies of this book or inquire about our quantity discounts for schools, hospitals, and affiliated organizations, contact us at 1-800-999-6884.

From our *Special Kids in School*® series

Taking A.D.D. to School
Taking Arthritis to School
Taking Asthma to School
Taking Autism to School
Taking Cancer to School
Taking Cerebral Palsy to School
Taking Cystic Fibrosis to School
Taking Depression to School
Taking Diabetes to School
Taking Down Syndrome to School
Taking Dyslexia to School
Taking Food Allergies to School
Taking Hearing Impairment to School
Taking Seizure Disorders to School
Taking Speech Disorders to School
Taking Tourette Syndrome to School
Taking Visual Impairment to School
...and others coming soon!

From our *Healthy Habits for Kids*® series

There's a Louse in My House
A Fun Story about Kids and Head Lice

From our *Special Family and Friends*™ series

Allie Learns About Alzheimer's Disease
A Family Story about Love, Patience, and Acceptance
Patrick Learns About Parkinson's Disease
A Story of a Special Bond Between Friends
Dylan Learns About Diabetes
A Story of Support and Understanding

And from our *Substance Free Kids*® series
Smoking STINKS!!™
A Heartwarming Story about the Importance of Avoiding Tobacco

Other books available now!
SPORTSercise!
A School Story about Exercise-Induced Asthma
ZooAllergy
A Fun Story about Allergy and Asthma Triggers
Rufus Comes Home
Rufus the Bear with Diabetes™
A Story about Diagnosis and Acceptance
The ABC's of Asthma
An Asthma Alphabet Book for Kids of All Ages
Trick-or-Treat for Diabetes
A Halloween Story for Kids Living with Diabetes

The Braille Alphabet

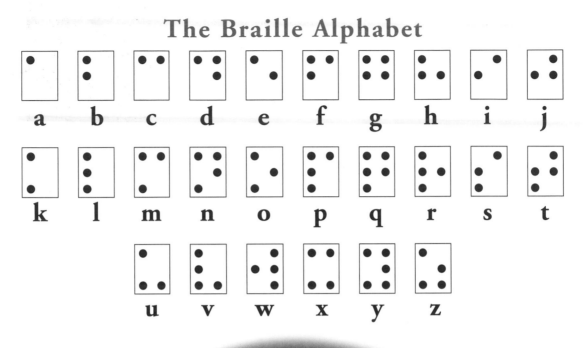

a b c d e f g h i j
k l m n o p q r s t
u v w x y z